Learning to Pray

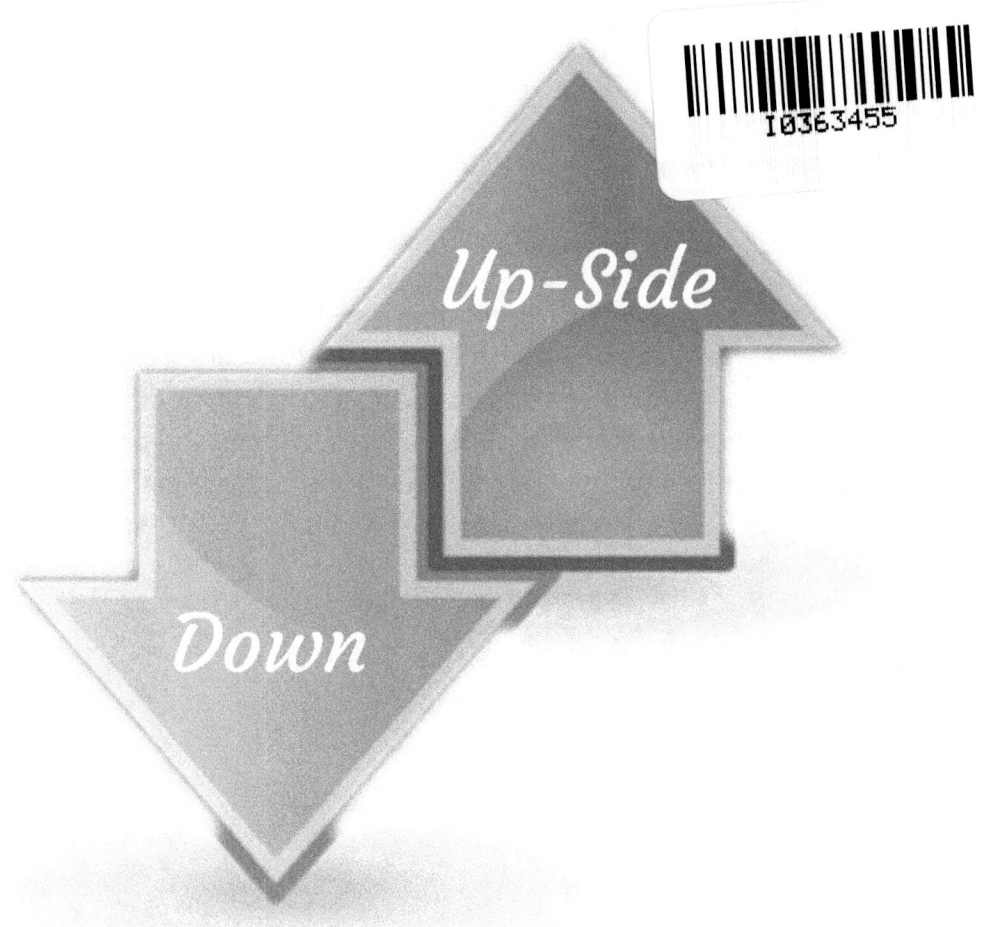

15- Week Bible Study Guide

Conflict Begins

Kingdom Life

Suit Up

Pray Upside Down - Rock Pifer (Author)

Copyright © 2021 by Abiding Line Publishing LLC

All rights reserved.

www.abidingline.com

No part of this publication may be reproduced, distributed, or transmitted in any form or by any means, including photocopying, recording, or other electronic or mechanical methods, without the prior written permission of the publisher, except in the case of brief quotations

Printed in the United States of America

"Scripture quotations taken from the (NASB®) New American Standard Bible®, Copyright © 1960, 1971, 1977, 1995, 2020 by The Lockman Foundation. Used by permission. All rights reserved."

www.lockman.org

DEDICATION

God uniquely inspires each of our spiritual journeys. He has a beautiful way of intersecting our paths with godly influencers; everyone has a part in teaching, encouraging, challenging, and directing our steps along the way.

I dedicate this small volume to those who have been patient, understanding, and kind, always pointing me to Jesus; for them, I am eternally grateful.

CONTENTS

Preface i

Introduction iv

Conflict Begins

Lesson 1	Getting Started	1
Lesson 2	Who is the Devil?	7
Lesson 3	War – Satan's Strategy	13
Lesson 4	God's Character and Strategy	19
Lesson 5	Our Place in the Kingdom	25

Kingdom Life

Lesson 1	Into the Heavenly Realm	32
Lesson 2	Lord, Teach us to Pray	38
Lesson 3	Search Our Heart, Lord	44
Lesson 4	Deeper Lord, Search Me	48
Lesson 5	Holy Spirit, Who Are You?	61

Suit Up

Lesson 1	Armor of God Part 1	71
Lesson 2	Armor of God Part 2	78
Lesson 3	Armor of God Part 3	85
Lesson 4	Keys to the Kingdom	91
Lesson 5	Our Mission	96

Facilitating a Small Group 103

PREFACE

Welcome to the *Learning to Pray Upside Down* Bible Study — 2nd Edition. I'm so excited for you to begin. A wonderful journey of discovery lies ahead.

This Bible study is for everyone, for the new follower of Jesus, a real eye-opening revelation of truth, and for the seasoned Christian, a rediscovery of the awesome nature of our God and our relationship to Him.

This Bible Study is designed for use in a small group setting. As you work through the study guide, allow ample time for discussion along the way. Encourage questions and observations.

If you are leading a small group, do your best to get everyone to participate in the study. In the back of this booklet, you will find helpful tips for facilitating a small group.

This Bible study is uniquely designed to help you see your life from a heavenly perspective; it will change your perception of your standing in Christ forever.

The Bible declares in Ephesians 2:6 - **"and raised us up with Him, and seated us with Him in the heavenly places in Christ Jesus."**

As followers of Jesus, we transferred into His kingdom, and through this Bible study, you are about to learn how to operate from there, from the **UPSIDE - DOWN**.

The **"Learning to Pray Upside Down"** study series contains the following titles:

Conflict Begins

Kingdom Life

Suit Up

We begin our journey together in part one, **"Conflict Begins,"** by going all the way back to the beginning, The **Book of Genesis**, rediscovering how it all began.

We examine the devil, and some of the reasons he fell from his powerful position in heaven, gaining new insight into his motivation to deceive Adam and Eve. We study his character, his scope of influence, along with his strategy and tactics.

In this study, we discover the awe-inspiring power and character of our God, along with **His** strategy, and we learn that our position in God's Family is secure; we are **"seated with Christ in the heavenly places."**

In part two, **"Kingdom Life,"** we head deeper into the **Heavenly Realm**.

We become aware of this astonishing truth; we are expressing God's Manifold Wisdom to the powers and principalities in the heavenly realms.

We begin to realize that our journey with Jesus is so much more than the salvation of our souls, but is a participation in His Glorious work, advancing His Kingdom here on earth.

We take a fresh look at the importance of prayer, and learn that the **"Lord's Prayer"** is a model for us to follow, not simply a prayer to recite.

Using Scripture, we will thoroughly examine our hearts, preparing for a **Baptism of the Holy Spirit**. We will learn how to operate with the power of the Holy Spirit in our lives.

In the final study guide, *Suit Up*, we explore the full Armor of God: what each piece is, how to wear it effectively, and how to ensure a proper fit.

After we put on the **Whole Armor of God**, we examine the **Keys to the Kingdom** and learn what they unlock.

And finally, we will rediscover our mission, the very reason that God called us into His Kingdom, and has equipped us so completely.

So, let's get started!

Introduction

My experience in pastoral ministry took place in rural Pennsylvania; nestled in the mountains of Cameron County, the heart of the Pennsylvania Wilds.

Like many small rural communities, the one my wife Sherri and I served had more than its fair share of problems. Having lived in the community for many years, we knew in detail the problems associated with the town: problems of drugs, alcoholism, suicide, and sexual abuse.

As pastors in this community, we saw firsthand the hurt and pain the devil had inflicted, and we began earnestly to pray for the deliverance of this town.

For years, every Sunday morning, Sherri and I would head to an overlook with a stunning view of our little town — and pray together.

On one particular occasion, I went alone and began praying over the town; what happened that day would change my life forever!

I stood there and began praying intensely against the powers and principalities that had been enslaving the people in my community.

Determined to see a breakthrough, I was passionately praying aloud, fists punching at the sky, as if pounding on the devil himself!

It was then that the most unexpected thing happened; the Lord seemed to draw very near, I could sense His Presence, and while I was praying, He asked me a question. To the best of my recollection, here is how the conversation unfolded.

The Lord said to me, "Rock, what are you doing?"

I was taken aback; it seemed obvious to me what I was doing, so I humbly answered the Lord, "I am praying."

He said in a gentle tone, "Why are you praying like that, punching at the sky?"

I was not sure what He was getting at, and I really did not know how to answer, so I responded, "This is how I do it."

There was a pause, and then he asked me another question: "Rock, where are you?"

I was growing even more confused, and all I could do was whisper, "I'm here, Lord." There was another pause, and then He rephrased the same question,

"Rock; spiritually, where are you?"

I responded by saying, "I'm with you, Lord." It was then that a Scripture from Ephesians 2:6 (And God raised us up with Christ and seated us with him in the heavenly realms in Christ Jesus) came rushing to my heart.

The Lord asked me again, "Rock, where are you?"

I responded, "I am seated with Christ in the heavenly realms." What the Lord said next would forever change my life and ministry!

The Lord said to me, "Rock, stop praying with your fists pounding at the sky, as if you were fighting an enemy that you are in subjection to. Instead, start praying from your true position in Me. Instead of praying with a down-side up mentality, pray from the up-side down; from the heavenly realm where you are seated; the battle is not over your head, but is under your feet."

Wow, stunned by what had just taken place, I realized that much of my prayer life happened without recognizing the authority with which one could pray.

I learned that I have authority and that I can pray expecting powerful answers. That day on the mountain changed everything!

It was this encounter with the Lord on that mountain that gave birth to **Praying Upside Down** — and, consequently, the name of our ministry, **Faith Upside Down**.

The Learning to Pray Upside Down Bible Study will help you understand the truth of who you are in Christ, discover the powerful position you have, and experience new passion and power in your prayer life!

This Bible study will help you understand your key role in partnership with Jesus, your Lord. It is a joint venture with Him, as He commands His followers to advance

His Kingdom here on earth.

God's great hope for you is not simply the forgiveness of sins and a place in heaven when you die, but rather, He wants you totally restored in heart, mind, and soul *NOW!*

As you enter this amazing adventure with God, you soon recognize that you are part of something marvelous, something beyond your earthly perspective; you are transported into the heavens with Christ; you live, breathe, and find your being in Him!

> **"For in Him we live and move and exist, as even some of your own poets have said, 'For we also are His descendants"** Acts 17:28

As a child of God, Jesus gives His authority, His power, and His Love to you, so that you can operate as His ambassador while living on earth.

> **"Therefore, we are ambassadors for Christ, as though God were making an appeal through us; we beg you on behalf of Christ, be reconciled to God"**
> 2 Corinthians 5:20

Furthermore, as an ambassador of Christ, you have a mission; He said . . .

> "And Jesus came up and spoke to them, saying, "All authority in heaven and on earth has been given to Me. Go, therefore, and make disciples of all the nations, baptizing them in the name of the Father and the Son and the Holy Spirit, teaching them to follow all that I commanded you; and behold, I am with you always, to the end of the age."
>
> Matthew 28:18-20
>
> Engaging this astonishing partnership, there are a few things you need to be keenly aware of. Satan has indeed been defeated by Christ; however, Satan's influence and evil intentions are still very active today. You need to be alert and on guard.
>
> **"Be of sober spirit, be on the alert. Your adversary, the devil, prowls around like a roaring lion, seeking someone to devour. So, resist him, firm in your faith, knowing that the same experiences of suffering are being accomplished by your brothers and sisters who are in the world."**
>
> 1 Peter 5:8-9

Through this Bible study series, we examine our role in this endeavor. We look at the **"KEY"** players involved, and their motives; together we **UN-MASK THE STRATEGY OF OUR ENEMY**, and you learn how to properly use the weapons God has given you, so that:

> ". . . you will be able to resist on the evil day, and having done everything, to stand firm. Stand firm therefore . . ."
>
> Ephesians 6:13-14

To be effective in this relationship with Christ, you must understand your true position in Him.

> ". . . and raised us up with Him, and seated us with Him in the heavenly places in Christ Jesus" Ephesians 2:6

Too often, we engage the enemy from a **"DOWN SIDE-UP"** mentality; feeling that the powers and principalities we engage are overhead, above our vantage point; beyond our ability and reach.

When engaging the enemy, it is not enough to know about our true position in Christ; we **MUST BELIEVE IT TO BE TRUE**!

> "The one who has the Son has the life; the one who does not have the Son of God does not have the life. These things I have written to you who believe in the name of the Son of God, so that you may know that you have eternal life." 1 John 5:12-13

It is imperative that by faith, you believe **EVERYTHING** God has said about you.

Assured of your salvation and your acceptance into His family, you begin to understand these truths as you explore the Word of God.

Prayer is the way we communicate with the God who redeemed us; it is how Jesus Himself talked to His Father, and His disciples noticed.

> "It happened that while Jesus was praying in a certain place, when He had finished, one of His disciples said to Him, "Lord, teach us to pray, just as John also taught his disciples.
>
> Luke 11:1

Since prayer was the only thing the disciples asked Jesus to teach them, it must be supremely important. The disciples saw what Jesus did; all the miracles He performed, and it was all somehow related to prayer.

Regarding the importance of prayer, as we begin this study, we must pray as the Apostle Paul did, asking that we receive the Spirit of wisdom and revelation so we may know Him better!

Read the following passage Paul penned to the Church in Ephesus.

> "For this reason, I too, having heard of the faith in the Lord Jesus which exists among you and your love for all the saints, do not cease giving thanks for you, while making mention of you in my prayers; that the God of our Lord Jesus Christ, the Father of glory, may give you a spirit of wisdom and of revelation in the knowledge of Him. I pray that the eyes of your heart may be enlightened, so that you will know what is the hope of His calling, what are the riches of the glory of His inheritance in the saints . . . "
>
> Ephesians 1:15-18

The apostle Paul longed for the people to get to know God more and more. It burdened him so much that he even declared in this passage, "I keep asking."

Paul never stopped praying this prayer for those people, and the reason is clear. The Spirit of wisdom and revelation we seek comes by way of God the Father. We do not grasp these truths by our own volition, but by God Himself.

Therefore, before every lesson, take time to pray, asking God the Father to open your eyes and your heart, to receive the Spirit of wisdom and revelation, so that you may know Him more!

PRAY!

Learning to Pray

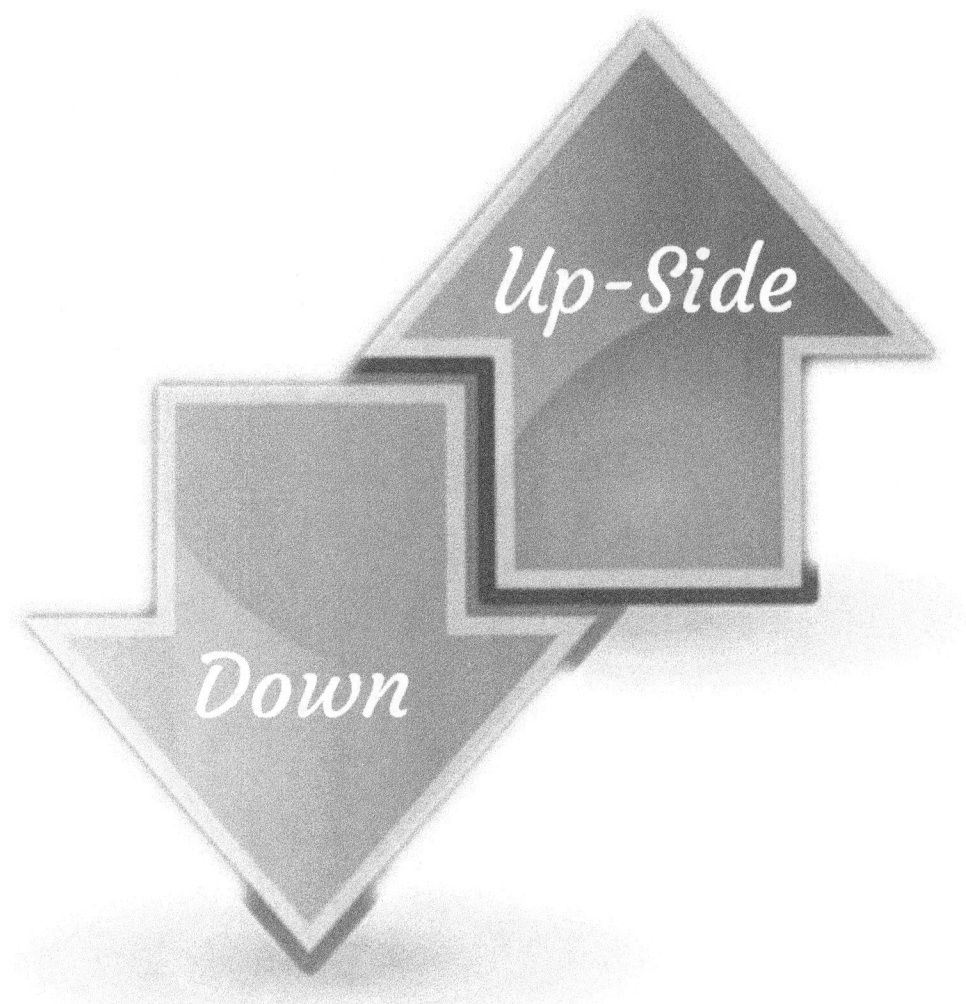

Conflict Begins

LESSON 1 – GETTING STARTED

Reading the introduction of this study, you learned of my encounter with God on the mountain and my conversation with Him.

- ❖ Have you ever heard from God?

- ❖ How did He speak to you?

- ❖ Was it an audible voice?

Take a moment and talk about your experiences listening to the voice of God with each other in your group.

God speaks to us in various ways; He is capable of impressing His thoughts and ideas in ways that are much louder than audible words.

Without question, the Scriptures will be the number one way in which God will speak to you. The Bible declares, **"all Scripture is God-breathed. . ."**

When reading Scripture, avoid reading it just for the sake of reading, but rather ask God to talk to you through His Word.

As you work through this study, you will encounter dozens of Scripture references related to each topic; take your time to look up each verse, talking to each other about what you find.

Approaching Scripture this way will produce wisdom and insight, as you learn and grow together.

So, to grasp the whole picture, we need to go back, all the way back, to the beginning.

1) Read Genesis 1:1-27 in the beginning, who created the heavens and the earth?

2) Who do you suppose the "Let Us" refers to in Genesis 1:26?

3) Read the following verses: Who specifically is the Creator?

John 1:1-17 / Colossians 1:13-16

4) According to Job 38:4-7, was there anyone else present while God created the heavens and the earth, and if so, who were they?

> "When the morning stars sang together - This must refer to some intelligent beings who existed before the creation of the visible heavens and earth: and it is supposed that this and the following clause refer to the same beings; that by the sons of God, and the morning stars, the angelic host is meant; as they are supposed to be first, though perhaps not chief, in the order of creation. For the latter clause the Chaldee has, "All the troops of angels." Perhaps their creation may be included in the term heavens, Genesis 1:1 "In the beginning God created the heavens and the earth." These witnessed the progress of the creation; and, when God had finished his work, celebrated his wisdom and power in the highest strains."
>
> Adam Clarke – Commentary on the Bible

From the Scripture in Job 38:4-7, it is reasonable to believe that in the very beginning, as God was creating the earth and forming man from the dust of the earth, the angels of heaven were present, watching, even wondering, what all of this meant.

5) According to Genesis 1:31, when God saw all that He had created, what did He think of it?

6) Read Genesis 2. What took place in this chapter?

7) How did man receive life?

We can see by taking a brief look at the Biblical account of the creation that Jesus Christ is the Creator.

> "... for by him all things were created: things in heaven and on earth, visible and invisible, whether thrones or powers or rulers or authorities; all things were created by him and for him"
> Colossians 1:16

We also learned that everything HE created was "VERY GOOD." When God had finished the creation, it was perfect, sinless, just as He intended, but something happened . . .

8) In Chapter 3, of the Book of Genesis, it describes what we refer to as "the fall of man." The chapter begins with a reference to what creature?

9) Read Revelation 12:9 and Revelation 20:2 who is the serpent.

10) What was the devil trying to do with Eve?

11) Read the following Scripture, John 8:44. Who is the father of lies?

→ Let's Talk About It ←

The plan of the devil seems to have worked; Eve was deceived, and Adam joined in too. We can learn some valuable lessons here.

How do you think Eve knew about the forbidden fruit?	Genesis 2:15-18
When Eve answered the devil, was she accurate in her answer?	Genesis 3:1-3
How important is it to memorize God's Word correctly?	Matthew 4:1-11

---

12) In Genesis 3:6-7, we see that Adam and Eve became aware of their nakedness, and in verse 8, they hid from God. Why do you think they hid?

13) In Genesis 3:9-13, we read an interesting dialogue between Adam, Eve, and God. What were Adam and Eve trying to do here?

14) Read Genesis 3:14-15. What creature does verse 15 refer to?

Satan, often referred to as the "old serpent" that deceived Adam and Eve, experienced defeat by Jesus Christ, the "Offspring" of the woman.

Satan would bruise Christ's heel—a non-fatal wound; but Christ would bruise Satan fatally, on the head!

Isaiah prophesied the first part of this proclamation: Jesus was "wounded and crushed for our sins" (Isaiah 53:5). Paul, writing after the Cross, proclaims the second part (Romans 16:20): "The God of peace will soon crush Satan under your feet."

In this lesson, we recalled the origin of sin as it relates to humanity. Adam and Eve chose to believe a lie perpetrated by the devil, and ignored God's warning; by doing so, they brought upon themselves and their descendants the misery we know as sin.

We also learned of the plan God initiated through Jesus, a plan that would redeem the brokenness and despair about to visit humanity.

In the following lesson, we discover more about Satan, the perpetrator of this hideous deception, and the reason for his hatred of God and especially for the people God created.

NOTES:

Lesson 2 – Who is the Devil?

In the first lesson of this Bible Study, we reviewed the creation account and humanity's fall into sin. It was necessary to go over this material to build a foundation and to revisit these essential truths.

In this lesson, we will begin to understand the nature of one of the primary players in this spiritual war.

SATAN, LUCIFER, THE DEVIL

1) Read Ezekiel 28:12-19. Bible scholars have referred to this passage of Scripture as a description of Satan. How does verse 12 describe the king of Tyre?

2) In verse 13, where was he?

3) In light of these verses, is the King of Tyre a human being, or not?

4) Satan; was he created, or did he always exist?

5) Read verses 14-15. How close to God do you think Satan was before he fell?

6) How beautiful was he?

7) Look up 2 Corinthians 11:14. Does Satan retain any of that original beauty?

8) Read Isaiah 14:12-14; Here we read of the "fall" of Lucifer, or Satan.

THE 5 "I WILLS" OF LUCIFER

> "But you said in your heart, ' I will ascend to heaven; I will raise my throne above the stars of God, and I will sit on the mount of assembly in the recesses of the north. I will ascend above the heights of the clouds; I will make myself like the Most High.
>
> Isaiah 14:13-14

I will _____

I will _____

I will _____

I will _____

I will _____

Let us examine some possible motivations behind these statements, the very reason for the "FALL" of Satan.

We have already learned that Satan was a created being, perfect in every way. Satan had direct access to God Himself, yet when God revealed His desire to create humanity, it seems as though Satan became infuriated.

The angels were present when God created the heavens and the earth; Job 38:4-7. Therefore, it makes sense that the most beautiful and wisest angel of them all was there too! It also noted that God does not hide His plans, but has revealed them for all to see and know.

GOD'S PLAN FOR MAN

Look up the following Scriptures, then compare what God's Word declares to be true of us and our position with Him, and contrast these with the five declarations Satan made; can you see any similarities?

Ephesians 2:6 / Revelation 3:21 / Hebrews 12:22-23

1 Thessalonians 4:16-17 / Genesis 1:27

It is interesting to note that God's plan for man tends to mirror some of the declarations made by Satan. Mankind would be much closer to God than he was.

According to the Scriptures on the previous page

We will   be seated in the heavens with Christ

We will   sit on Christ's throne with Him

We will   come to Mount Zion (general assembly)

We will   be caught up in the clouds

We will   be created in the image of God

Could it be that when Satan saw this new creation of beings, **"created a little lower than the angels,"** (Psalm 8:5) having a place in heaven, closer to God than his own, he rebelled?

Could it be that he felt no one was as qualified as he was to have this place in heaven? His pride and arrogance would not allow anyone, or anything else, to eclipse him.

→ Let's Talk About It ←

Satan's argument must have been persuasive. Revelation 12:4 declares that a third of the stars of heaven were swept out along with him, a reference to a third of the angels in heaven cast out with Satan.
Why do you think his argument was so convincing?

Do you think the other angels are still curious about this?

Satan is on a mission to destroy all that God has made, especially mankind. This is the very reason he tempted Eve, and managed to get his sin, planted into the heart of man. While his plan seems to have worked, God had already established a redemptive plan for humanity.

10) According to Ephesians 1:4, when did God's plan for the redemption of man begin?

11) Read Ephesians 2:6. At what point in time are believers seated with Christ?

We are beginning to see just how much God was looking ahead, planning for our redemption. His plan would unfold, and it would be a stunning success, in spite of the devil's best efforts to thwart those plans.

In the next lesson, we will uncover some of the tactics and strategies Satan loves to use.

Notes:

Lesson 3 – War – Satan's Strategy

As we have been learning, this "spiritual conflict" began before the creation of mankind. Since the angels were present before our creation, they also knew the plan God had for mankind as well.

Battle lines have been drawn, and an ongoing spiritual war, now fought in the heavenly realm, a war we must participate in, and the stakes are high!

Satan's rebellion against God's plan and subsequent deception foisted on humanity initiated the conflict.

In this lesson, we examine the strategy of our enemy. If the devil has a plan, and we understand it, we will be in a much better position to fight when the attacks come.

> "But one whom you forgive anything, I also forgive; for indeed what I have forgiven, if I have forgiven anything, I did so for your sakes in the presence of Christ, so that no advantage would be taken of us by Satan, for we are not ignorant of his schemes."
>
> 2 Corinthians 2:10-11
>
> "No wonder, for even Satan disguises himself as an angel of light."   2 Corinthians 11:14
>
> "You are of your father the devil, and you want to do the desires of your father. He was a murderer from the beginning, and does not stand in the truth because there is no truth in him. Whenever he tells a lie, he speaks from his own nature, because he is a liar and the father of lies"
>
> John 8:44

THE DEVIL'S CHARACTER

Satan is a _____ and a _____
                              John 8:44

Satan is a _____
                        Genesis 3:4 / Revelation 12:9

Satan is an _____
                              Revelation 12:10

SATAN'S CHARACTER - OPPOSITE OF JESUS

Satan is an accuser   →   **Jesus is an Advocate**   1 John 2:1

Satan is a murderer   →   **Jesus is the Life**   John 14:6

Satan is a lair   →   **Jesus is the Truth**   John 14:6

THE DEVIL'S AUTHORITY AND TERRITORY

1) According to Luke 4:5-7, what territory does he have authority or rule over?

2) What does the devil have according to Revelation 12:12?

3) How does Ephesians 2:2 describe the devil?

4. Read 1 John 5:19; who controls the world?

> → **Let's Talk About It** ←

Are believers under the control of the devil?

What is "the world" as it relates to this Scripture, 1 John 5:19?

We have discovered the devil does have a great deal of authority over "the world." This authority, coupled with his angst for God and mankind, has caused Satan to become a formidable enemy.

We will continue our study and look at some of the "schemes" our adversary loves to use.

THE DEVIL'S SCHEMES & TACTICS

"The god of this age has blinded the minds of unbelievers, so that they cannot see the light of the gospel of the glory of Christ, who is the image of God"

2 Corinthians 4:4

---

5) Where does Satan do his most effective work?

6) Why is it important for Satan to "blind" the mind?

7) According to 1 Thessalonians 3:5, what is one scheme of Satan?

8) Reading 2 Corinthians 11:3, we see another tactic. What is it?

WEAPONS THE ENEMY USES

9) Read 2 Corinthians 6:14-18. Are we to be "yoked" with unbelievers?

10) What do righteousness and lawlessness have in common?

11) "Belial" is a reference to Satan. What do Satan and Jesus have in common?

Satan's primary weapon used against the Christian is to get the Christian involved with such things as darkness, lawlessness, idols, unbelievers, gossip, etc.

(We MUST be involved with unbelievers, BUT NOT the activities they indulge in)

If Satan can get Christians involved with these things, the Christian becomes ineffective and unable to stand against further attacks.

? Brainstorm and list some of the other weapons that Satan might try to use against us. _____
_____
_____
_____

→ Let's Talk About It ←

On the one hand, the Bible calls us to share our faith and our life with unbelievers, yet tells us not to be yoked with them. This seems to be a paradox.

Can you think of some practical ways to reach the lost, without becoming yoked to them?

What should we do if already yoked to an unbeliever, perhaps through marriage?

See 1 Corinthians 7:12-16

We can see clearly that Satan has considerable influence in our society. His malevolent intentions are evident the world over.

We must remain vigilant and on guard, keeping our minds clear of distractions; otherwise, we fall into sin, becoming ineffective in our prayer, and even becoming a tool in the hands of our enemy.

God has a plan and strategy too, and it involves us; in the next lesson, we look at the character attributes of God and begin discovering His plan.

Notes:

Lesson 4 – God's Character & Strategy

We studied the character traits of Satan, our enemy, and looked at his authority base, examining his tactics and the weapons he uses.

It would appear that he has quite an array of **"weapons"** and **"schemes."** That is true; without question, he is a formidable opponent, and we should treat him with caution, but not fear.

God also has a plan; today, we will begin looking at **His character**, **His authority**, **His tactics**, and **His weapons**.

GOD'S PLAN IS PERFECT, unmarred by sin, and His plan includes us.

We begin by examining just a few of the character attributes of God.

The character descriptions of God are nearly as endless as our vocabulary. Those mentioned here will give us an idea of the awesome nature of our God.

THE CHARACTER OF GOD

God is _____
Exodus 3:14 / Acts 17:24-25 / John 5:26

God is _____
Psalm 102:25-27 / Malachi 3:6

God is _____
Psalm 90:2 / Revelation 1:8

God is _____
1 John 3:20 / Psalm 139:16

God is _____
Job 12:13 / Romans 11:33

God is _____
1 John 4:16 / Romans 5:8

God is _____
Isaiah 6:3 / Psalm 99:9

God is _____
Deuteronomy 9:7-8 / John 3:36

God is _____
Deuteronomy 32:4 / Isaiah 45:19

THE AUTHORITY OF GOD

God has the authority to _____
Matthew 9:6

God has the authority to _____
Luke 4:35-36

God has the authority to _____
John 10:17-18

God has **SUPREME AUTHORITY** over all of creation; everything is subject to **HIS** authority. Any authority that Satan has is because God has granted it to him.

We are beginning to get a view of **God's character** and **HIS AUTHORITY** over creation. Compared to the characteristics and authority of Satan, we can only marvel at **GOD'S MAJESTY;** there is no comparison at all!

WHAT HAPPENED AT THE CROSS

At the Cross, Jesus **"CRUSHED"** Satan

Defeated _____
1 John 3:8 / 2 Corinthians 5:21

Defeated _____
Isaiah 53:4-5 / Psalm 103:1-3

Defeated _____
Hebrews 2:14 / 1 Corinthians 15:51-57

Defeated _____
John 12:31 / Revelation 11:15

> "For he has rescued us from the dominion of darkness and brought us into the kingdom of the Son he loves, in whom we have redemption, the forgiveness of sins"
>
> Colossians 1:13-14

1) According to the above Scripture, from what did Jesus rescue us?

2) A transfer took place. What was it, and why was this significant?

→ **Let's Talk About It** ←

How much hold does the kingdom of darkness have on us?

How do we recognize the kingdom of darkness?

If we engage in "dark" activities again, what effect will it have?

> "Behold, I give you the authority to trample on serpents and scorpions, and over all the power of the enemy, and nothing shall by any means hurt you"
>
> Luke 10:19

3) Who is giving us authority in this Scripture?

4) What do serpents and scorpions represent?

5) How much of the enemy's power do we have authority over?

AUTHORITY – "The power to enforce laws, exact obedience, command, determine, or judge."

~ More verses revealing God's Authority given to believers ~

> "And He summoned the twelve and began to send them out in pairs, and gave them authority over the unclean spirits" Mark 6:7
>
> "For though we walk in the flesh, we do not wage battle according to the flesh, 4 for the weapons of our warfare are not of the flesh, but divinely powerful for the destruction of fortresses. We are destroying arguments and all arrogance raised against the knowledge of God, and we are taking every thought captive to the obedience of Christ." 2 Corinthians 10:3-5
>
> What then shall we say to these things? If God is for us, who is against us? Romans 8:31

We have studied the reasons that we find ourselves engaged in a spiritual conflict. We have uncovered some of the **"MOTIVES"** that drive our enemy into action, and we have looked at a few of his tactics. We are beginning to understand the true nature of our enemy, and of our **"Advocate"** Jesus Christ.

We have examined the **AUTHORITY** that God has given us. We need to clearly understand this authority, looking deeper into our true standing in Christ. The following lesson reveals our true position in God's family.

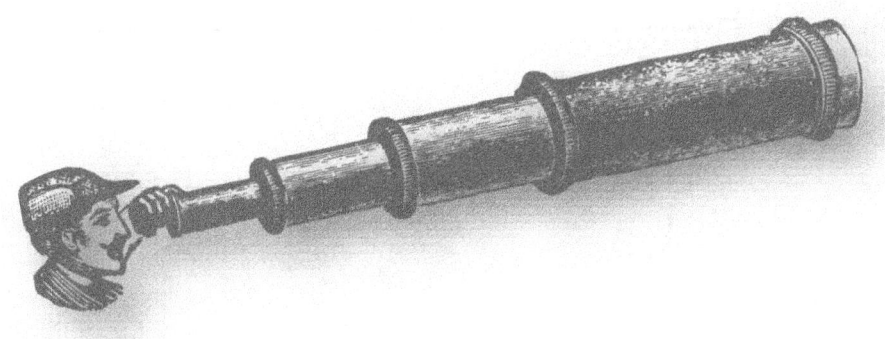

Notes:

Lesson 5 – Our Place in the Kingdom

In this lesson, we will examine just where we fit in, as it relates to the Kingdom of God; what you learn here may change your outlook on life forever!

OUR POSITION

1) Where do our "Spiritual Blessings" come from?   Ephesians 1:3

2) Who gives these blessings, and did we get it all?   Ephesians 1:3

3) When did God choose us?   Ephesians 1:4

4) What is our relationship to God?   Ephesians 1:5

Adoption -   "To take into one's family through legal means and raise as one's own child."

"The adopted child is treated by law as the natural child of the adopting parents, upon the entry of the final adoption decree. The adopted child, therefore, gains the right to inherit from the adoptive parents and adoptive parents' relatives. . ."

(Adoption Information Clearinghouse)

5) What do we have through Jesus` blood?   Ephesians 1:7

6) When are we included in Christ?   Ephesians 1:13

7) When we believed, what happened?   Ephesians 1:13-14

The truths that we are about to explore **CANNOT** be understood, apart from direct revelation by the **HOLY SPIRIT**.

We **NEED** to be able to take hold of these truths in order to apply them to our lives.

Once again, read the Scripture below, feel the heart of the apostle Paul. He desires that the people of God would receive the **SPIRIT OF WISDOM AND REVELATION**.

> "I keep asking that the God of our Lord Jesus Christ, the glorious Father, may give you the Spirit of wisdom and revelation, so that you may know him better. I pray also that the eyes of your heart may be enlightened in order that you may know the hope to which he has called you, the riches of his glorious inheritance in the saints"
>
>   Ephesians 1:17-18

We have prayed this prayer before; we need to pray it again!

PAUSE & PRAY!

8) When Christ rose from the dead, where did He go?   Ephesians 1:20

9) The position Jesus Christ received placed Him above what, and for how long does He maintain this position?   Ephesians 1:21

10) Who is the head of the church?   Ephesians 1:22

Reading these Scriptures, we understand the depths of the POWER and AUTHORITY, Jesus our Lord now encompasses; we feel a sense of awe, and humility at His glorious position!

11) Again, where are we in relation to Christ?   Ephesians 2:6

12} When will this event take place?   Ephesians 2:6

> Our *CURRENT* location: *SEATED with CHRIST in the HEAVENLY REALMS*, we do not wait for a future event, as we are already there! Praise the Lord!

13. Why would God do this?   Ephesians 2:7

We now know our true position in Christ; seated with Him in the heavenly realms. We have also learned that, as adopted sons and daughters, we have all the legal rights that a natural-born child would have.

We are truly a part of the Family of God. The family Name is ours, along with all the "CLOUT" it carries.

Conflict Begins - Summary

We began our journey together by going all the way back to the beginning, The Book of Genesis, rediscovering how it all began.

We examined the devil and some of the reasons he fell from his powerful position in heaven. We gained new insight into his motivation to deceive Adam and Eve. We examined his character, his scope of influence, along with his strategy and tactics.

We studied the overwhelming power and character of our God, along with His strategy, and we learned that our position in God's family is secure; we are "seated with Christ in the heavenly realms."

In the second study guide in this series, "Kingdom Life," we will head deeper into the Heavenly Realm, learning more about prayer, and we will have a deep and profound searching of our hearts before God.

We will understand who the Holy Spirit is and what He intends to do with and through us. Get ready, prepare your heart, for a Baptism of the Holy Spirit!

Notes:

Learning to Pray

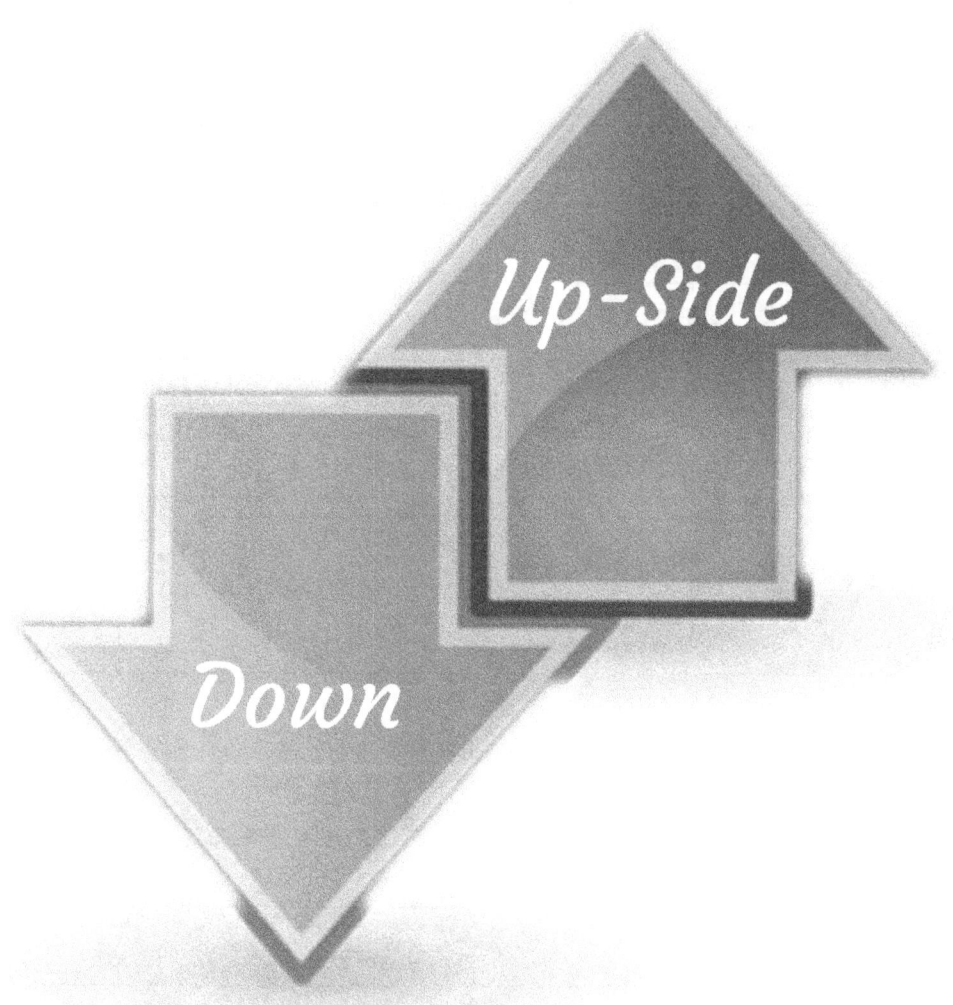

Kingdom Life

We began our journey together in the first study guide in this series, "Conflict Begins," by going all the way back to the beginning, The Book of Genesis, rediscovering how it all began.

We examined the devil and some of the reasons he fell from his powerful position in heaven, gaining new insight into his motivation to deceive Adam and Eve. We studied his character, his scope of influence, along with his strategy and tactics.

In the first study, we discovered the awe-inspiring power and character of our God, along with His strategy, and we learned that our position in God's family is secure; we are "seated with Christ in the heavenly realms."

In part two, "Kingdom Life," we head deeper into the Heavenly Realm. We will become aware of this astonishing truth; we are expressing God's Manifold Wisdom to powers and principalities in the heavenly realms.

We realize that our journey with Jesus is so much more than the salvation of our souls; it is a participation in His Glorious work, advancing His Kingdom here on earth.

We take a fresh look at the importance of prayer, and learn that the "Lord's Prayer" is a model for us to follow, not simply a prayer to recite.

Using Scripture, we thoroughly examine our hearts, preparing for a Baptism of the Holy Spirit. We learn how to operate with the power of the Holy Spirit in our lives.

Lesson 1 – Into the Heavenly Realm

We begin our study **"Kingdom Life"** by heading into the Heavenly Realm. You are about to uncover a mystery that may change your outlook on Christianity forever! Again, as we learned to do in **"Conflict Begins,"** pray for the Spirit of Wisdom and Revelation to guide us, so our spiritual eyes open, able to grasp these deep truths.

THE PURPOSE

> **"To me, the very least of all saints, this grace was given, to preach to the Gentiles the unfathomable riches of Christ, and to enlighten all people as to what the plan of the mystery is which for ages has been hidden in God, who created all things; so that the multifaceted wisdom of God might now be made known through the church to the rulers and the authorities in the heavenly places. This was in accordance with the eternal purpose which He carried out in Christ Jesus our Lord, in whom we have boldness and confident access through faith in Him."**
>
> Ephesians 3:8-12

1) What is the "mystery" that Paul is referring to? READ ALSO- Romans 11:33 / 1 Peter 1:10-12 / 1 Corinthians 2:7-10

This passage of Scripture talks about **"Multifaceted Wisdom."** In order to understand these words, look carefully at the Greek word and its meaning for **"Manifold."**

> POLUPOIKILOS   (pol-oo-poy'-kil-os)
>
> "much variegated, a great variety of colors, of cloth or a painting, multi-faceted like a diamond."

2) According to the Greek word and definition given above, describe in your own words what **"multifaceted wisdom"** means.

3) To whom is the multifaceted wisdom directed?

4) How does God intend to express this wisdom?

→ Let's Talk About It ←

God chose us, His church, to express this multifaceted wisdom to the "rulers and authorities in the heavenly realms."

What are the implications of this truth, and what is your part in expressing it?

Why do you think He did this?

We begin to see the passionate desire of God to involve us, His chosen children, to express His multifaceted wisdom to the rulers and authorities in the heavenly realms.

God has a plan, not only for us, but for all of His creation, including the angels in heaven, and that plan is unfolding, even as we engage in this study.

We are on display and the powerful forces in the heavenly realm are watching God's plan unfold with increasing interest.

This facet of Christianity is central to the church, yet often overlooked. We focus so much attention on getting people redeemed and involved in church activities.

As important as it is to help people find faith in Christ for salvation, we now see that it is just the beginning; there is so much more! The heavens are intently watching God's plan unfold.

> "... Even angels long to look into these things." — 1 Peter 1:12

God's marvelous plan is taking effect, and we must willingly participate. When we stop to consider what God has chosen to do with us, we get an awesome feeling of responsibility and one of great assurance.

THE HOPE

Let us examine the prayer the apostle Paul had for the church in Ephesus, looking at his heart's desire for the people of God.

> "**For this reason I bend my knees before the Father,** [15] from whom every family in heaven and on earth derives its name, [16] that He would grant you, according to the riches of His glory, to be strengthened with power through His Spirit in the inner self, [17] so that Christ may dwell in your hearts through faith; and that you, being rooted and grounded in love, [18] may be able to comprehend with all the saints what is the width and length and height and depth, [19] and to know the love of Christ which surpasses knowledge, that you may be filled to all the fullness of God.
>
> [20] Now to Him who is able to do far more abundantly beyond all that we ask or think, according to the power that works within us, [21] to Him be the glory in the church and in Christ Jesus to all generations forever and ever. Amen."
>
> Ephesians 3:14-21

5) From whom do we get our Name?

6) What is Paul asking in verse 16?

7) How is it that Christ dwells in our hearts?

8) In verses 18-19 Paul is trying to describe the Love of God. How does he describe it?

9) Can we really describe God's Love?

10) According to verse 20, how much is God able to do?

→ Let's Talk About It ←

How would you describe the love of God to someone seeking answers to the Christian faith?

In this lesson, we have a glimpse of the magnitude of God's Kingdom, and it is stunning! We are not only invited in; we are on full display for the **"powers and principalities"** to view and consider.

It is as if the heavenly hosts are still curiously watching the plans of God unfold, and God has confidence in us to reveal His wisdom to them.

Life in the Kingdom is very different from what we are accustomed to here on earth. We notice quickly that there are still powerful enemies prowling around, and we discover that, in and of ourselves, we are at a tremendous disadvantage.

However, God's plan does not leave us dangling from a precipice; but rather, He draws us in, even closer to Him than we ever could imagine.

From here, we move into the battle, learning how to pray from our true position in Christ. We truly will learn to pray, **"Up-Side Down."**

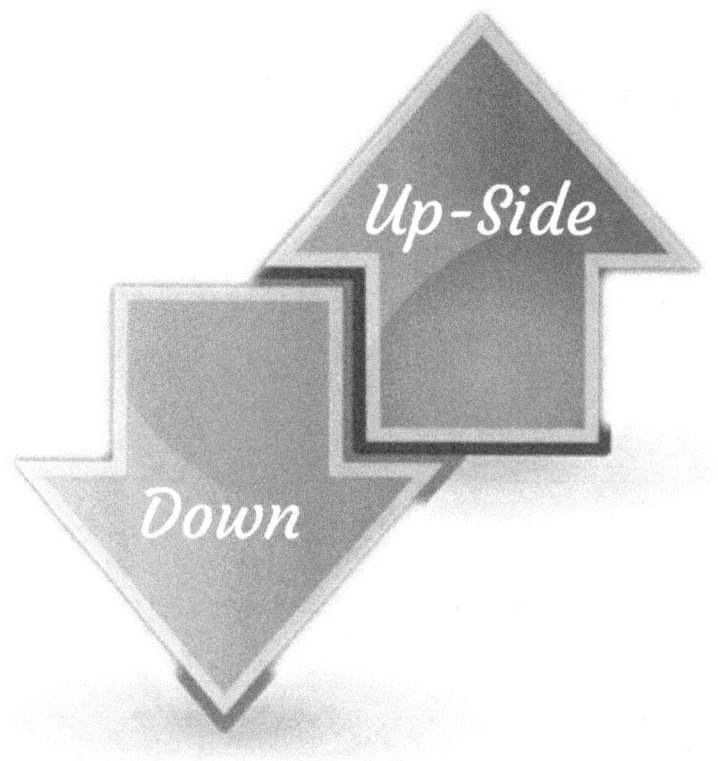

Notes:

Lesson 2 – Lord, Teach Us to Pray

We have learned the true nature of our enemy and the awesome nature of our God! We also have learned of our true position and our standing with God.

We are adopted children, with all the rights of a natural-born child. We learned that we are "seated with Christ in the heavenly realms."

As we prepare to learn more about engaging the enemy and being effective in spiritual battle, we need to look at what exactly it means to "PRAY." Since spiritual battles are fought through prayer, we need to grasp these essential truths.

Prayer Defined

"a privilege and an obligation of the Christian, where we communicate with God. It is how we convey our confession (1 John 1:9), requests (1 Timothy 2:1-3), intercessions (James 5:15), and thanksgiving (Philippians 4:6) to our holy God. We are commanded to pray (1 Thessalonians 5:17)

Some personal requirements of prayer are a pure heart (Psalm 66:18), belief in Christ (John 14:12-14), and that the prayer is according to God's will (1 John 5:14).

We can pray standing (Nehemiah 9:5), kneeling (Ezra 9:5), sitting (1 Chronicles 17:16-27), bowing (Exodus 34:8), and with lifted hands" (1 Timothy 2:8).

PRAYER

> "It happened that while Jesus was praying in a certain place, when He had finished, one of His disciples said to Him, "Lord, teach us to pray, just as John also taught his disciples." And He said to them, "When you pray, say:
>
> Father, hallowed be Your name. Your kingdom come. Give us each day our daily bread. And forgive us our sins, for we ourselves also forgive everyone who is indebted to us. And do not lead us into temptation."
>
> Luke 11:1-4

1) What was Jesus doing when the disciples found Him?

2) Was prayer important to Jesus?

Matthew 14:23 / Matthew 26:36 / Mark 1:35 / Mark 6:46
Luke 5:16 / Luke 6:12 / Luke 22:40

→ Let's Talk About It ←

Jesus is the Son of God, and according to the Scriptures, Jesus is God incarnate, in other words, God in the flesh!

Why did He need to pray?

---

3) Back to Luke Chapter 11, when the disciples found Jesus, what did they ask Him?

4) What do you think motivated the Disciples to ask Jesus this question?

5) In Matthew 6:9-13, Jesus begins the prayer slightly differently than in Luke 11. What is the significance of Jesus including the word "Our" in this passage?

→ Let's Talk About It ←

Why is community prayer so important?

Acts 2:1-4 / Acts 4:31 / Matthew 18:19-20

---

6) According to verse 2, where is the Father?

7) What does "Hallowed" mean?

8) When Jesus says to pray, "Your Kingdom Come," what do you think He means?

Psalm 45:6 / Psalm 103:19 / Psalm 145:11-13 / Isaiah 9:6-7

9) In verse 3, we are to pray that God's "what" be done.

10) Look up the following verses; list some of the elements of "God's Will" you find.

Jeremiah 29:11 / 1 Timothy 2:3-4 / 1 Thessalonians 5:18 / 1 Thessalonians 4:3 / Luke 9:23

Proverbs 3:5-6 / 1 Peter 2:15 / Ephesians 5:15-20 / 2 Peter 3:9 / 1 John 1:9 / 1 Timothy 2:4

_____

_____

_____

_____

_____

_____

_____

These are just a few examples of God's will; there are many more contained in the Scriptures. It is our responsibility as followers of Jesus to learn and to know His will.

As you become a life-long student of God's Word, His will becomes clearer and more evident. Commit to reading and studying His word every day!

11) We are to pray also for our daily bread. What other things do you think can be included here?

12) In verse 4, we are to ask God to forgive us our sins, for we also forgive those who sin against us. How important is it for us to forgive?

Matthew 6:14-15 / Mark 11:25 / Luke 17:3-4 / Colossians 3:13

13) Finally, in verse 4, we are to ask God to lead us not into temptation, but to deliver us from the evil one. Do you think God would lead you into temptation?

Jesus gives us this **MODEL PRAYER** as a guide. Rather than simply reciting this prayer, use it to help inform and mold your own personal prayer.

As we learn to pray, we need to keep this MODEL in front of us. It will help keep us focused. Our highest aim in prayer, and especially spiritual warfare prayer, is to bring God's Kingdom to earth, so that His ways become our ways.

When we pray, "Your Kingdom Come," we are engaging the enemy. We are asking God to bring His Kingdom authority to the places we live, work, and play.

When the Kingdom of God begins to take root and advance, our enemy, Satan, is quite distraught, and he will do all he can to stop the advancement. Satan looks for weaknesses in us so he can exploit them. He wants our prayer to be ineffective.

In the next two lessons, we are going to examine our hearts for some of those weaknesses. It will be a reflective time, possibly painful at times. We need God to search our hearts.

> "Search me, God, and know my heart; test me and know my anxious thoughts."
>
> Psalm 139:23

Notes:

Lesson 3 – Search Our Heart, Lord

> **Search me, God, and know my heart; test me and know my anxious thoughts. See if there is any offensive way in me, and lead me in the way everlasting."**
>
> Psalm 139:23-24

1) What does the Scripture say about sin and its effect between us and God?

   Psalm 66:18 / Isaiah 59:1-2 / John 9:31

2) What else could hinder our prayers?

   Proverbs 21:13 / Isaiah 1:15-17 / 1 Peter 3:7

3) According to James 4:17, what is sin?

4) According to 1 John 1:9; if we sin what must we do?

5) According to 1 John 1:9, what does God promise to do if we do our part?

→ Let's Talk About It ←

How would you describe the need to "confess your sins," what do you think it means?

What are some ways in which God will purify you from all unrighteousness?

Read Psalm 51 carefully. In this Scripture, King David bares His heart before God. David has sinned, and he recognizes the awful rift it has created between himself and God.

6) What is the first thing David asks for?

7) Can we say that we do not know our sin?

8) Where does God desire truth?

9) David does not want to lose what?

10) Sin brings the loss of what?

11) Believing that God would restore him, what does David say he will do?

Sin can prevent God from hearing and acting on our prayers. Satan loves to exploit these weak areas of our lives; he often provides temptations and will do everything in his power to get the Christian to sin.

When we get complacent in our walk with Jesus, we let down our guard; little sins, shoved aside and ignored, become huge obstacles to our prayer life.

Remember, temptation is NOT sin, acting on the temptation is.

God has given us a promise regarding temptation, and it is a verse worthy of memorization.

> **"No temptation has overtaken you except something common to mankind; and God is faithful, so He will not allow you to be tempted beyond what you are able, but with the temptation will provide the way of escape also, so that you will be able to endure it."**
>
> 1 Corinthians 10:13

In our next lesson, we are going to look at several reflective questions, asking ourselves if we have any areas of unconfessed sin that we need to deal with.

I strongly encourage you to FAST and PRAY as you review the following lesson; this can be intense, but necessary. Remember . . .

"The word of God is living and active, and sharper than any two-edged sword, even penetrating as far as the division of soul and spirit, of both joints and marrow, and able to judge the thoughts and intentions of the heart. The Word of God is sharper than any two-edged sword."

We must allow the Word of God to do its work in our hearts.

Notes:

Lesson 4 – Deeper Lord, Search Me!

TIME FOR REFLECTION

The following lesson is designed to help us know our own heart; it is an assignment every follower of Jesus should do from time to time.

The Bible declares:

> **"If I had cherished sin in my heart, the Lord would not have listened"**
> Psalm 66:18
>
> **"If anyone turns a deaf ear to my instruction, even their prayers are detestable."**
> Proverbs 28:9
>
> **"And when you stand praying, if you hold anything against anyone, forgive them, so that your Father in heaven may forgive you your sins."** Mark 11:25
>
> **Husbands, in the same way be considerate as you live with your wives, and treat them with respect as the weaker partner and as heirs with you of the gracious gift of life, so that nothing will hinder your prayers."** 1 Peter 3:7

The Bible is clear; if we harbor sin, nurture it, and ignore it, then God will NOT hear us! There is one way to reach the depths of our heart, and that is by allowing the Holy Spirit to use the Word of God to search us.

> "For the word of God is alive and active. Sharper than any double-edged sword, it penetrates even to dividing soul and spirit, joints and marrow; it judges the thoughts and attitudes of the heart." Hebrews 4:12

Reflections

The questions posed here are very deep and searching. If the Holy Spirit reveals weak areas in your life, areas of sin, be sure to take the steps necessary to make it right.

Confess (agree with God that you have sinned) and repent (determine in your heart not to do this again) and walk victoriously.

---

1 Thessalonians 5:18

"in everything give thanks; for this is the will of God for you in Christ Jesus."

- ❖ Do you worry about anything?
- ❖ Have you failed to thank God for all things, things that seem bad, along with those that are good?

Ephesians 3:20

"Now to Him who is able to do far more abundantly beyond all that we ask or think, according to the power that works within us"

- ❖ Do feelings of inferiority keep you from serving God?
- ❖ Do you feel that you have no talent to give God?

Reflections

Acts 1:8

"But you will receive power when the Holy Spirit has come upon you; and you shall be My witnesses both in Jerusalem and in all Judea, and Samaria, and as far as the remotest part of the earth."

- ❖ Have you failed to be a witness for Christ with your life?
- ❖ Have you felt it was enough to live your Christianity at home, neglecting the command to reach the ends of the earth?
- ❖ Do you support your local church missions' efforts?

Romans 12:3

"For through the grace given to me I say to everyone among you not to think more highly of himself than he ought to think; but to think so as to have sound judgment, as God has allotted to each a measure of faith."

- ❖ Do you insist on your own rights?
- ❖ Do you tend to have a superior attitude toward others in Christ?
- ❖ When God wants to change you, do you rebel?

Reflections

Ephesians 4:31

"Get rid of all bitterness, rage and anger, brawling and slander, along with every form of malice."

- ❖ Do you complain, find fault, and argue?
- ❖ Do you have a critical spirit?
- ❖ Do you carry a grudge against other Christians because they do not see eye to eye with you on all things?

1 Corinthians 6:19

"Do you not know that your body is a temple of the Holy Spirit, who is in you, whom you have received from God? You are not your own."

- ❖ Are you careless with your body?
- ❖ Do you eat too much? Are you a glutton?
- ❖ Are you sexually active with those you are not married to?

Reflections

Ephesians 4:29

"Do not let any unwholesome talk come out of your mouths, but only what is helpful for building others up according to their needs, that it may benefit those who listen."

- ❖ Do you use foul language and laugh at vulgar and coarse jokes?
- ❖ Do you engage in gossip?
- ❖ Do you have a critical spirit?

Ephesians 4:27

"and do not give the devil a foothold."

- ❖ Do you open the door for Satan by engaging in psychic predictions, horoscopes, and other practices contrary to God's Word?
- ❖ Do you doubt God's Word?
- ❖ Are there people you refuse to forgive?

Reflections

1 Corinthians 8:9

"Be careful, however, that the exercise of your freedom does not become a stumbling block to the weak."

- ❖ Do you abuse your freedoms in Christ?
- ❖ Do you consider your weaker brother or sister in the Lord; are you a stumbling block?

Hebrews 10:25

"Let us not give up meeting together, as some are in the habit of doing, but let us encourage one another--and all the more as you see the Day approaching."

- ❖ Are you sporadic in church attendance?
- ❖ Do you avoid others of faith?
- ❖ Do you evade accountability?

Reflections

Colossians 3:9

"Do not lie to each other, since you have taken off your old self with its practices."

- ❖ Do you exaggerate the truth and tell little white lies?
- ❖ Do you tell things the way you want them told, rather than the way they are?
- ❖ When someone genuinely asks how you are doing, are you truthful?

1 Peter 2:11

"Dear friends, I urge you, as aliens and strangers in the world, to abstain from sinful desires, which war against your soul."

- ❖ Do you have a lustful eye towards the opposite sex?
- ❖ Do you read romance novels, watch pornography, or fill your mind with unholy ideas?
- ❖ Do you get envious of those who have more material wealth than you?
- ❖ Do you secretly wish evil upon others?

Reflections

John 13:35

"By this all men will know that you are my disciples, if you love one another."

- ❖ Are you secretly pleased over the misfortunes of another?
- ❖ When a service project to reach your community begins, do you make yourself scarce?
- ❖ Would you rather give money than give your time and yourself to a neighbor?

Colossians 3:13

"Bear with each other and forgive whatever grievances you may have against one another. Forgive as the Lord forgave you."

- ❖ Have you failed to forgive anybody anything they might have said or done against you?
- ❖ Have you purposely turned certain people off because they offended you?

Reflections

Ephesians 4:28

"He who has been stealing must steal no longer, but must work, doing something useful with his own hands, that he may have something to share with those in need."

- ❖ Do you steal from your employer by doing less work than you should?
- ❖ Do you resist tithing on your income?
- ❖ Do you steal music, videos, and software from the internet?

Ephesians 5:16

". . . making the most of every opportunity, because the days are evil."

- ❖ Do you waste time; are you lazy?
- ❖ Do you spend too much time watching TV, surfing the internet, Facebook, and Twitter?
- ❖ Are you procrastinating?

Reflections

Matthew 6:24

"No one can serve two masters. Either he will hate the one and love the other, or he will be devoted to the one and despise the other. You cannot serve both God and Money."

- ❖ Are you trying to make as much money as you can?
- ❖ Do you accumulate material things?
- ❖ Have you withheld God's share of money from him?

Matthew 23:28

In the same way, on the outside you appear to people as righteous but on the inside you are full of hypocrisy and wickedness.

- ❖ Do you know in your heart that you are a counterfeit, acting to be a real Christian, when in fact, you are not?
- ❖ Are you hiding behind church membership to cover a life still full of sin?
- ❖ Are you the person in your home who you are on Sunday morning in church?

Reflections

Philippians 4:8

"Finally, brothers, whatever is true, whatever is noble, whatever is right, whatever is pure, whatever is lovely, whatever is admirable--if anything is excellent or praiseworthy--think about such things."

- ❖ Do you enjoy listening to gossip, and passing it on?
- ❖ Do you believe rumors or partial truths about an enemy or competitor?
- ❖ Do you feel good inside when someone "gets what's coming to them?"

James 2:17-18

In the same way, faith by itself, if it is not accompanied by action, is dead. But someone will say, "You have faith; I have deeds." Show me your faith without deeds, and I will show you my faith by my deeds.

- ❖ Do you avoid getting your hands "dirty" waiting for someone else to meet an obvious need?
- ❖ Do you pass up opportunities to share your faith; meet the needs of the poor, or serve your local church, because you simply do not want to?

Allowing the Scriptures to search our hearts can be a very revealing exercise and can even be quite painful; and this for a good reason; God judges the heart!

> **"For the word of God is living and active, and sharper than any two-edged sword, even penetrating as far as the division of soul and spirit, of both joints and marrow, and able to judge the thoughts and intentions of the heart"**
>
> Hebrews 4:12
>
> "All the ways of a person are clean in his own sight, but the Lord examines the motives."
>
> Proverbs 16:2
>
> "But the Lord said to Samuel, "Do not look at his appearance or at the height of his stature, because I have rejected him; for God does not see as man sees, since man looks at [b]the outward appearance, but the Lord looks at the heart."
>
> 1 Samuel 16:7

It is crucial that we consent to the deep searching of our heart by the Holy Spirit; the stakes are high, and the battle we are in has eternal consequences.

We must not hide anything from God, submitting to His authority in ALL things.

These previous two lessons have helped to prepare us for an encounter with the Holy Spirit. In the following lesson, we are going to learn about the amazing Holy Spirit. We now come to Him with clean hearts and minds, ready to encounter Him in a fresh, new and powerful way!

Notes:

Lesson 5 – Holy Spirit, Who are You?

In our last segment, we allowed the Holy Spirit to use the Scriptures to examine our hearts, revealing anything that would hinder our walk with God.

It is the hungry heart; the searching heart, which longs to be "filled" with the inexpressible and powerful presence of the Holy Spirit. When we search our hearts, we soon find, in and of ourselves, no good thing prevails.

> "I said to the Lord, 'You are my Lord; I have nothing good besides You." — Psalm 16:2

When we recognize our spiritual deficit, we hunger to be "satisfied - filled" with righteousness as the Bible declares:

> "Blessed are those who hunger and thirst for righteousness, for they will be satisfied." — Matthew 5:6

In this lesson, we look at who the Holy Spirit is, and how we can be "Filled with the Spirit."

> Spiritual Warfare is NOT for the "CARNAL" Christian, but rather for those who have studied their own hearts, and who long to be empowered by the Holy Spirit. For those who, by an act of their will, have chosen to be "crucified with Christ," they will be filled with the Holy Spirit. (Galatians 2:20)

So, let us begin our journey of discovery, as we seek to know the fullness of the Holy Spirit. We want to know Who He is, and what He would like to do with us.

Quite often, descriptions we have heard regarding the Holy Spirit come across as a "force" or a "thing," rather than a person. Let's discover who He really is.

The Holy Spirit _____
Acts 13:2

The Holy Spirit _____
Romans 8:14

The Holy Spirit _____
John 15:26

The Holy Spirit _____
John 16:13

The Holy Spirit _____
Acts 16:6-7

The Holy Spirit _____
Acts 20:28

The Holy Spirit _____
Romans 8:26

The Holy Spirit _____
John 16:8

The Holy Spirit _____
Ephesians 4:30

The Scriptures reveal that the Holy Spirit commands, guides, leads, convicts, and grieves.

"The Holy Spirit is beyond doubt, a Person."

1) In the following Scriptures, how does the Bible portray the Holy Spirit?
John 14:16 / John 14:26 / John 15:26 / John 16:7

> The Greek word used to describe the Holy Spirit is:
> Parakletos par-ak'-lay-tos intercessor, consoler: - advocate, comforter.

2) What are some of the purposes of the Holy Spirit outlined in John 16:7-11?

The Holy Spirit can teach, comfort, console, lead, convict, and so much more! Without the power and presence of the Holy Spirit in our lives, we will be ineffective in Spiritual Warfare.

The Holy Spirit, being One with the Father and the Son, empowers us to live victorious Christian lives. Apart from the Holy Spirit, we operate in our own strength and are prone to frequent defeat.

We must be "Filled with the Spirit."

> "I am the vine, you are the branches; the one who remains in Me, and I in him bears much fruit, for apart from Me you can do nothing."   John 15:5

THE HOLY SPIRIT – "BE FILLED."

3) According to Acts 1:4-8, what did Jesus tell His disciples to do?

4) Read the following Scriptures, and tell what happened to the people involved?
    Acts 2:4 / Acts 4:31 / Acts 8:15-17 / Acts 9:17 / Acts 19:2-6

5) The seven sons of Sceva had a problem. What was it?   Acts 19:13-16

6) Is it optional for the Christian to "Be Filled with the Holy Spirit?" Ephesians 5:18

7) How does a person receive the Holy Spirit?   Luke 11:9-13

8) Who gives the Holy Spirit?   Luke 11:9-13

10) How do we receive any promise that God gives?
    Ephesians 2:8-9 / Acts 3:16 / Romans 1:17 / Romans 3:28 / Romans 4:16
    2 Corinthians 5:7 / Galatians 3:14 / Hebrews 11

> **→ Let's Talk About It ←**
>
> Would God command you to do something impossible?
>
> What would keep a person from being filled with the Holy Spirit?
>
> What prevents YOU from being filled with the Holy Spirit right now?

Everything we receive from God comes by faith. Find a quiet place, take the Scripture from Luke 11:9-13, and open it up before God. Read the passage, reminding God of the promise, and your need to Be Filled with the Holy Spirit.

Ask Him to fill you, and by faith, receive.

Avoid seeking a sign from God, but rather seek HIM; signs will come as He chooses. Too often, those seeking to be "filled" look for an experience, or some form of manifestation to "prove" they are filled; this often becomes a hindrance, because the focus is off of God and onto ourselves.

The Holy Spirit fills you when you receive Him by faith; walk in that faith, and God Himself will show you "great and mighty things you know not of" Jeremiah 33:3.

We cannot underestimate the importance of being filled with the Holy Spirit and your total reliance on Him. He is your leader, and we DO NOT act alone!

Congratulations, you have completed **"Kingdom Life."**

You are now aware of this astonishing truth; you are expressing God's Manifold Wisdom to the powers and principalities in the heavenly places. You realize that your journey with Jesus is so much more than the salvation of your soul; it is a participation in His Glorious work of advancing His Kingdom.

You have a fresh view of the importance of prayer, and have learned that the "Lord's Prayer" is a model to follow.

You examined your heart deeply and learned how to operate with the power of the Holy Spirit in your life. All of this knowledge is very important as it relates to praying, and especially spiritual warfare prayer. You are now praying "Up-Side Down."

In the following, and final study in this series, "Suiting Up," we examine the full ARMOR OF GOD.

We are going to learn what this armor is, how to wear it effectively; making sure we have a good fit.

After we put on the Whole Armor of God, we are going to examine the "Keys to the Kingdom" that we now possess, and finally, we will learn our mission.

Time to suit up!

Notes:

Learning to Pray

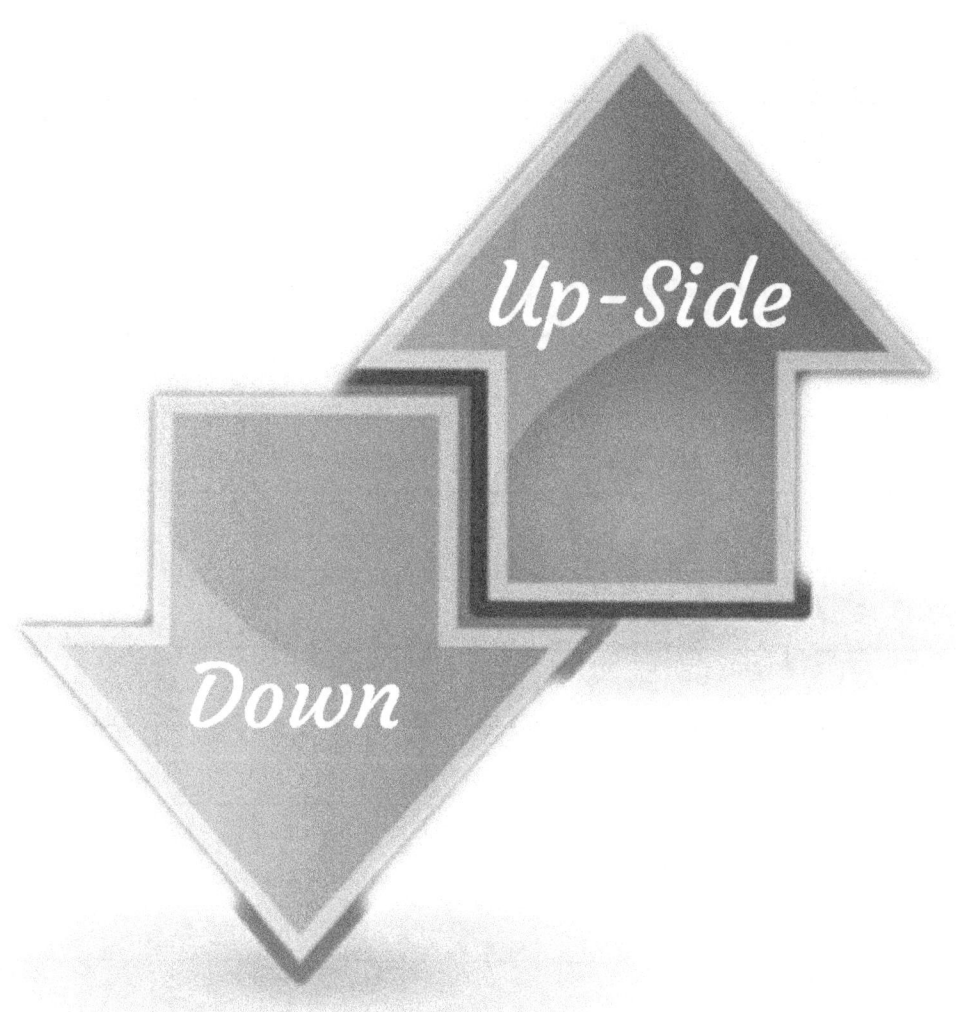

Suit Up

Preface

We began our journey together in the first study guide in this series, **"Conflict Begins,"** by going all the way back to the beginning, The Book of Genesis, rediscovering how it all began.

We examined the devil, and some of the reasons he fell from his powerful position in heaven, gaining new insight into his motivation to deceive Adam and Eve. We studied his character, his scope of influence, along with his strategy and tactics.

In the first study, we discovered the awe-inspiring power and character of our God, along with His strategy, and we learned that our position in God's family is secure; we are "seated with Christ in the heavenly realms."

In the second study guide, **"Kingdom Life,"** we headed deeper into the Heavenly Realm.

We became aware of this astonishing truth; we are expressing God's Manifold Wisdom to the powers and principalities in the heavenly realms.

We realized that our journey with Jesus is so much more than the salvation of our souls, but it is a participation in His Glorious work, advancing His Kingdom here on earth.

We took a fresh look at the importance of prayer, and learned that the "Lord's Prayer" is a model for us to follow, not simply a prayer to recite.

Using Scripture, we thoroughly examined our hearts, preparing for a Baptism of the Holy Spirit. We learned how to operate with the power of the Holy Spirit in our lives.

In the final study guide, **"Suit Up,"** we examine the full Armor of God. We learn what this armor is and how to wear it effectively, ensuring a good fit.

After we put on the Whole Armor of God, we examine the Keys to the Kingdom and learn what they unlock.

Finally, we will rediscover our mission, the very reason that God called us into His Kingdom, and has equipped us so completely.

So, let's get started!

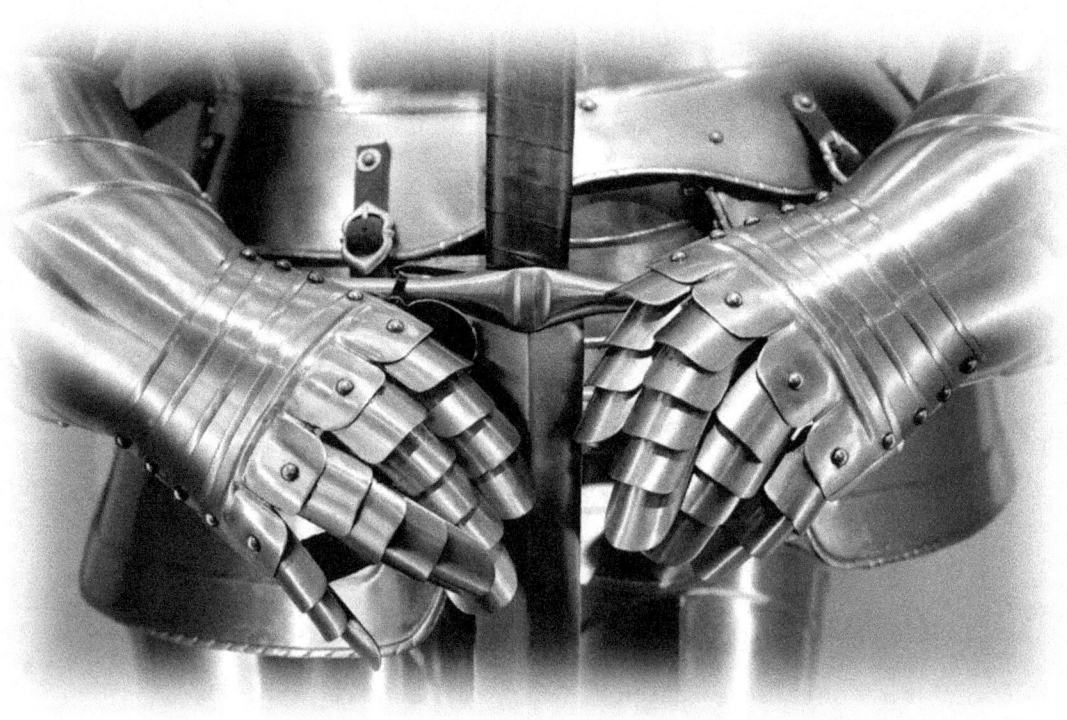

Lesson 1 – Armor of God Part 1

In this study guide, **"Suit Up,"** we are going to learn about the ARMOR OF GOD, and what it protects.

We will examine each article, gaining valuable insight into the wisdom of God, as He so graciously has provided us with everything we need to be effective and protected as we engage our enemy.

We will also discover the **"keys to the kingdom"** that Jesus talked about, and finally, we will discover our mission.

So, let us begin with the ARMOR OF GOD and the Greek word used.

> Panoplia - p an-op-lee'-ah; full armor ("panoply").

1) What does the armor of God consist of?   Ephesians 6:13-17

_____   _____

_____   _____

_____   _____

→ Let's Talk About It ←

When police officers and soldiers purchase bulletproof vests and other body protective devices, who is responsible for the quality of the materials provided?

Who is responsible for the quality of the armor of God?

Can we be confident that the armor of God will be effective?

In the time of the Apostle Paul's writing to the church in Ephesus, the Roman soldiers were on patrol throughout the area.

The Roman soldier wore armor to protect himself in battle. When Paul talked about putting on the whole armor of God, you can be sure the people immediately could relate to the armor Paul described.

BELT OF TRUTH

The "BELT" or "GIRDLE" fastened around the middle. The lower armor hung on the belt, and the sword often rested in a sheath attached to the belt.

The "BELT" was central to the armor of the Roman soldier, and the "BELT OF TRUTH" is central to the Christian's armor too. Everything hangs on this.

2) What is the guiding principle in all of the following verses?
Psalm 15:1-2 / Psalm 25:5 / Psalm 119:43

Psalm 145:18 / Proverbs 23:23

3) Speaking of Himself, what did Jesus say He was?   John 14:6

4) Satan loves to keep people in bondage, and one way to do that is to present half-truths and deceptions to the Christian. Jesus says something about the truth in the following Scripture. What does He say? John 8:32

5) What is truth? John 17:17

6) Can we grow in the truth? 2 Timothy 2:15

7) What did Jesus do when He responded to Satan's temptations?
Matthew 4:1-10

8) Read Luke 4:1-12. Satan used Scripture to tempt Jesus. Were his quotations of Scripture accurate, and did Satan use the Scripture in proper context?

9) Satan used Psalm 91:11-12 in his quote to Jesus; why do you think he left out verse 13?

Truth remains truth, as long as it is not manipulated or twisted in any way. Satan loves to take Scripture out of context and bend it to get his way, rather than God's way.

> *"Those choosing to manipulate Scripture to get their own way, will end up with the same fate as Satan."*

God expects us to walk in truth always, even if it may cause pain; we need to be truthful at all times. Someone once said, "What we keep from God, the devil is sure to get." Therefore, we must keep our hearts truthful at ALL times before God!

Satan, referred to as **"THE FATHER OF LIES,"** does some of his most crafty work in this area. Let's be careful not to give him a foothold, but rather buckle the BELT OF TRUTH firmly around our waist.

BREASTPLATE OF RIGHTEOUSNESS

The Roman soldiers also wore a breastplate. This piece of armor PROTECTED THE HEART and other vital organs from attack, and without this essential piece of armor, the soldier was vulnerable to a fatal strike.

For the Christian, the BREASTPLATE OF RIGHTEOUSNESS is indispensable; without this, we would be vulnerable to an attack as well, an attack of the heart!

Satan loves to accuse, cast doubt, and instill fear in the heart of the believer. Unless we have this covering over our hearts, his attacks may be successful!

10) How does God view all of our righteous acts done in our own strength?

Isaiah 64:6

11) What has Christ become for us?   1Corinthians 1:30

12) What do the following verses indicate we should do?

Romans 13:14 / 1 Corinthians 15:53 / Ephesians 4:24 / Colossians 3:10

"Just as David also speaks of the blessing of the person to whom God credits righteousness apart from works: "Blessed are those whose lawless deeds have been forgiven, and whose sins have been covered."   Romans 4:6-7

The Greek word for "forgiven" in the above verse is often translated "imputed" which means to designate any action or word or thing as reckoned to a person.

(1) the sin of Adam is imputed to all his descendants, i.e., it is reckoned as theirs, and they are dealt with therefore as guilty;

(2) the righteousness of Christ is imputed to them that believe in him, or so attributed to them as to be considered their own; and

(3) our sins are imputed to Christ, He assumed our "law-place," undertook to answer the demands of justice for our sins. In all these cases, the nature of imputation is the same.

Easton's Bible Dictionary

It is sometimes hard for us to believe that simply by placing faith in JESUS CHRIST, ALL our sins are forgiven, and we can stand before God as if we never did anything wrong.

Just like Abraham "believed God and it was credited to him as righteousness," we believe God too, and by faith, just like Abraham, we believe in the death, burial, and resurrection of Jesus Christ.

When we do this, God forgives sins, and we stand, not in our own righteousness but in the righteousness of Christ.

So, we "Put On Christ"; He is our Breastplate of Righteousness; we cannot go anywhere without Him! To go in our own righteousness is to go spiritually naked, vulnerable to deadly attacks from the enemy!

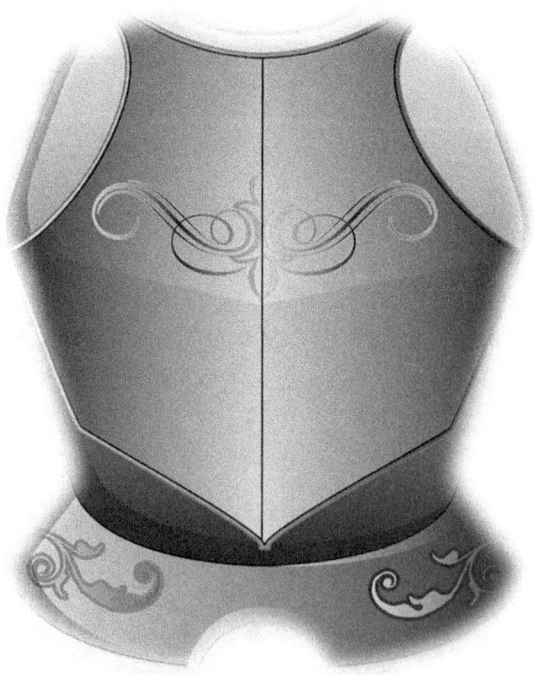

Notes:

Lesson 2 – Armor of God Part 2

In the previous lesson, we studied the "Belt of Truth" and the "Breastplate of Righteousness."

We discovered how essential these two pieces of armor are. Today, we examine a few more articles of armor we must be sure to put on before engaging our enemy!

FEET FITTED WITH THE PREPARATION OF THE GOSPEL OF PEACE

We are now going to get our feet fitted with a special pair of "GOSPEL SHOES." Following the Lord is not an easy task. The road may get difficult; "SERPENTS" and "SCORPIONS" need to be crushed along the way; hot desert places to walk through, and without the proper "SHOES" we could be bitten by these serpents and scorpions, and our feet will burn in the hot sand!

There will also be times when we will need to "STAND OUR GROUND," and we will need a solid footing, not moved by the enemy, and God always provides what we need.

1) According to the following verses, who causes us to be able to stand in difficult places? 2 Samuel 22:34 / Psalm 18:33

2) What do the following verses have in common?
Psalm 31:8 / Psalm 40:2 / Psalm 56:13 / Psalm 116:8 / Psalm 119:101 / Psalm 140:4

3) What is happening in the following verses?

    Psalm 44:5 / Psalm 60:12 / Psalm 108:13 / Malachi 4:3 / Luke 10:19

As you can see, our God can cause us to stand and give us shoes that will trample down our enemy. This is good news, but there is more. Once we have our feet fitted with shoes that are able to cause us to stand, and that have the ability to crush our enemy, we need to use these shoes to carry forward the incredible message of the Gospel of Peace.

4) How does Isaiah 9:6 describe the coming Messiah, Jesus?

5) According to Romans 5:1, what do we have with God?

6) What do the following Scriptures have in common?

    Psalm 29:11 / Psalm 85:8 / Proverbs 16:7 / Philippians 4:6-7

Matthew 5:9 declares, "Blessed are the peacemakers, for they will be called sons of God."

> The word used for "peacemaker" consists of two words:
> eirēnopoios   i-ray-nop-oy-os' / which means to be peaceable
> poieō   poy-eh'-o / which means; to bring forth; to continue; to keep

When we encounter a man or woman of God, one who has given themselves over to Jesus, filled with the Holy Spirit, we sense something about them. It is like a spiritual fragrance filling the air, a certain, tangible presence that something is profoundly right!

The reason for this is simple, yet profound. Apart from Jesus, we are at "enmity" with God, and there is no peace, only hostility. A person given over to Christ, filled with the Holy Spirit, is no longer at war with God or with others. They bring a sense of peace wherever they go!

When we walk with our feet fitted with the Gospel of Peace, we bring that kind of peace with us. No longer at war with God, but rather friends of God, the Peace of God follows us, and it is palpable.

→ Let's Talk About It ←

Can you identify someone who carries the peace of God wherever they go? What would prevent the Gospel Shoes of Peace from being "fitted" on YOUR feet?

SHIELD OF FAITH

7) What exactly is faith?   Hebrews 11:1

8) Where does faith come from?

    Ephesians 2:8-9 / Romans 12:3 / 1 Corinthians 12:9

9) Is it possible for faith to be developed?

    Romans 10:17 / 2 Corinthians 10:15 / Ephesians 4:13

10) Faith is essential to our walk with God. How important is it to have faith?

    Hebrews 11:6

11) Does everyone have the same level of faith?

    Mark 9:24 / Romans 12:3 / Romans 12:6 / Romans 14:1

Roman soldiers had shields that were made in such a way that they could be hooked together, creating a line of defense. We too can use our SHIELD OF FAITH to protect those who are weak and lacking.

→ Let's Talk About It ←

How strong and developed is your faith?

Are there any holes in your shield of faith?

Is there someone that you need to cover with your shield?

We see how important the **"SHIELD OF FAITH"** is to the rest of our armor. As we continue our study, we will discover a primary tactic Satan uses to inflict pain.

When Roman soldiers fought, they would often take their arrows and dip them in tar, setting them on fire before shooting at an enemy. If the arrow hit its mark, it would burn deeply into the flesh, causing great pain; often leading to further damage, by way of infection. The shield would protect the soldiers from these "missiles."

In the spiritual realm, Satan launches **"FIRE-TIPPED MISSILES"** at the Christian, trying to inflict pain and infection, knowing that if he can cause a deep hurt, the Christian may strike back; Satan is extremely cunning in this effort. The reason for his success is that frequently, when a Christian does strike back, they are directing their attack in the wrong direction.

When this happens, the attack from Satan has worked; our focus centers on a person, created in the image of God, rather than on the true perpetrator instigating the attack: Satan!

Read James 3:1-12 carefully and answer the following questions. . .

12) What does the tongue do in verse 5?

13) How does James describe the tongue in verse 6?

14) Are we able to tame the tongue according to verse 8?

15) According to verses 9 and 10, what does the tongue do?

> → **Let's Talk About It** ←
>
> Do you use your tongue in the manner we just discussed?
>
> Who is in control of your tongue?
>
> When someone talks about you, or gossips about you, do you retaliate?
>
> If you do retaliate, who do you think is motivating you to do it?

We already learned that one of Satan's primary tactics is to deceive. If he can get people to hurt another person by saying hurtful things, then he can just walk away, and the damage will continue long after he leaves. We must temper our tongue.

> "If you can't say it out of love, even if you're right, you're wrong."

Notes:

Lesson 3 – Armor of God Part 3

So far, we have studied the "Belt of Truth", the "Breastplate of Righteousness", the "Gospel Shoes of Peace", and the "Shield of Faith." We only have two articles left in our wardrobe that we need to wear in our spiritual battle, and they are the Helmet of Salvation and the Sword of the Spirit.

HELMET OF SALVATION

The helmet was a crucial component of the Roman soldier's fortification; it protected the head. You may recall seeing pictures of Roman soldiers with bright plumage on top of their helmets; this would often indicate which division, or regiment, the soldier belonged to.

Quite often, as soon as you saw the soldier's helmet, you knew who you were going to be fighting.

Certain Roman regiments had brutal and cruel reputations, and the very sight of the colorful plumage would cause some enemies to run for cover!

In the spiritual battle we engaged in, the Helmet of Salvation protects our minds.

1) According to the following verses, how are we to love God?

Matthew 22:37 / Mark 12:30 / Luke 10:27

2) Can the mind, focused on the "world" or on "carnal" matters, please God?

Romans 8:6-7

3) Can the mind be changed and renewed?   Mark 5:15 / Romans 12:2 / Ephesians 4:23

→ Let's Talk About It ←

Read Mark 8:31-33 and discuss the following:

Was Peter in his right mind?

Who was controlling his thoughts?

Could a Christian be manipulated by Satan through the mind?

Satan loves to manipulate and distort God's Word; he is a master of deception. Quite often, we will find his greatest deceptions have an element of truth to them. We must be on guard at all times.

4) Whose mind are we to have?   Corinthians 2:16

5) Is it possible for a group of people to be of one mind, and if so, why is it important?

Acts 4:32 / 1 Corinthians 1:10 / 2 Corinthians 13:11   Philippians 2:2 / 1 Peter 3:8

The Helmet of Salvation is vital; it helps to protect our minds from the continuous attempts by Satan to influence our thoughts. Salvation is not just redemption; it is also restoration, completeness, and a new sense of who we are.

> **"Therefore, if anyone is in Christ, this person is a new creation; the old things passed away; behold, new things have come."** 2 Corinthians 5:17

As we continue our study, we now look at the only offensive part of our armor, the Sword of the Spirit, which is the Word of God.

With the Sword of the Spirit, we will be able to advance with all authority and power.

SWORD OF THE SPIRIT

6) What does the following Scripture have to say about the Word of God?

Hebrews 4:12

The Word of the Lord is _____
Psalm 18:30

The Word of the Lord is _____
Psalm 33:4

The Word of the Lord is _____
1 Peter 1:25

The Word of the Lord is _____
Psalm 119:89

7) Can you trust the promises of God?

        2 Corinthians 1:20 / Proverbs 3:3-6 / Revelation 22:6

8) What should we do with the Word of God?

        Psalm 119:11 / Psalm 119:16

9) According to 2 Timothy 3:16, what is the Scripture useful for?

_____ _____

_____ _____

The Word of God is more than able to slay the enemy. We need to hide it in our hearts and learn to meditate on it, filling up with the whole counsel of God and not just the parts that make us feel good.

→ Let's Talk About It ←

Read 2 Corinthians 10:3-5 and talk about the following:

What would you consider a stronghold to be?

What kinds of things keep people away from God?

A Roman soldier needed to take careful aim, then thrust in the sword; they would practice those swordsmanship moves repeatedly, until it became second nature.

Likewise, we need to be careful students of God's Word, not wielding the Word of God carelessly, but rather studying, memorizing, and applying it; learning to use it wisely.

As we near the conclusion of this Bible Study, we need to consider what we are going to do with what we have learned.

How do we proceed, and what, exactly, are our orders?

In the following two lessons, we will discover the Keys we have been given, and finally, our Mission; all of which we receive and access through prayer, our direct communication line to God Himself.

Notes:

Lesson 4 – Keys to the Kingdom

In this lesson, we reveal the Keys to the Kingdom, learning how important they are in our journey with Christ.

We have covered a great deal through this study, and we are ready to engage, Full Force, the Kingdom advancing mission Jesus gives us. We start this lesson by listening in to a discussion Jesus had with His disciples.

> **Now when Jesus came into the region of Caesarea Philippi, He was asking His disciples, "Who do people say that the Son of Man is?" [14] And they said, "Some say John the Baptist; and others, Elijah; and still others, Jeremiah, or one of the other prophets." [15] He said to them, "But who do you yourselves say that I am?" [16] Simon Peter answered, "You are the Christ, the Son of the living God." [17] And Jesus said to him, "Blessed are you, Simon Barjona, because flesh and blood did not reveal this to you, but My Father who is in heaven. [18] And I also say to you that you are Peter, and upon this rock I will build My church; and the gates of Hades will not overpower it. [19] I will give you the keys of the kingdom of heaven; and whatever you bind on earth shall have been bound in heaven, and whatever you loose on earth shall have been loosed in heaven."**
>
> Matthew 16:13-19

1) When Jesus asked the disciples who they thought He was, Peter spoke up, saying, "You are the Christ, the Son of the living God." In Verse 17, who revealed this truth to Peter?

Jesus knew that His crucifixion was imminent and that He would soon return to the Father. When He spoke to Peter, He was revealing that He was about to give him the **Keys to the Kingdom**, a transfer was about to take place. The Scripture that was fulfilled in Christ was now going to be fulfilled in Peter and the Church that was about to be built.

SIX KEYS

 Gate Key – The Front Door

2) According to the following Scriptures, who alone grants entrance into the Kingdom of God?

John 6:44 / John 10:7-9 / Matthew 7:13-14 / Revelation 3:20

 The Key to the Family Name

3) Read the following Scriptures: What relationship do we now have with God?

Galatians 4:7-9 / Romans 8:15 / 1 John 3:1-21
1 John 3:2 / Philippians 2:15 / Galatians 3:26

 The Key to Kingdom Treasure

4) According to the following verses, are we to expect anything from God when we ask?

John 14:13 / John 14:14 / Matthew 21:22 / John 16:23-24
1 John 5:14 / John 15:16 / John 15:7 / Mark 11:24

🗝️ The Key to Authority

5) Review the following Scriptures: how much power and authority do those who follow Jesus have?

      Isaiah 54:17 / Luke 10:19 / 2Corinthians 10:5 / Matthew 28:18 / Mark 3:15
      Luke 9:1 / John 14:12 / Acts 1:8 / Eph 3:20 / Eph 6:10 / Heb 4:12

🗝️ The Key to the Armory

6) The following passage outlines the items in God's armory chest; what are they?

      Ephesians 6:10-18

→ Let's Talk About It ←

What are the Keys to the Kingdom?

When receiving a key, what is the implied expectation?

Would you give a key to someone unqualified to use it?

"Wait! I thought there were six keys."

There is one more **KEY**, and we have touched on it a little earlier in this study.

The last KEY is really the master KEY; it is a key that everyone has, and it is a powerful gift from God Himself!

> "For it is by grace you have been saved, through FAITH-and this is not from yourselves, it is the gift of God- not a result of works, so that no one can boast."
>
> Ephesians 2:8-9

What "KEY" do you find in this passage?

 _____

Everyone has the KEY of FAITH, a gift from God Himself; it is the MASTER KEY, giving access to all the other keys!

It is by FAITH that we believe in Jesus, and by FAITH, we open the door to Him, by FAITH, we experience the Baptism of the Holy Spirit, and by FAITH, we follow His commands. By FAITH, we access **ALL** of the promises of God, and by FAITH, we put on the full armor of God! It is by FAITH we exercise authority in Jesus Name, and by FAITH, we advance the Kingdom of God!

Faith is the master KEY!

The **Keys to the Kingdom** allow us access to the **Kingdom**, and we have received the **Family Name**, having access to all the **Treasures** belonging to the Family.

We also have the **Authority** that goes with the Family Name, and finally, we have the key to the **Armory**, able to access all we need to fight and to win!

Notes:

Lesson 5 – Our Mission

As we enter the last lesson in our Bible study, we discover once again what we already know to be true: God has commissioned us to advance His kingdom here on earth until His return.

Read again the following passage, penned by the great Apostle Paul, as he encourages the early church, regarding the availability of God's great power and authority.

> **"For this reason I too, having heard of the faith in the Lord Jesus which exists among you and your love for all the saints, ^{16} do not cease giving thanks for you, while making mention of you in my prayers; ^{17} that the God of our Lord Jesus Christ, the Father of glory, may give you a spirit of wisdom and of revelation in the knowledge of Him. ^{18} I pray that the eyes of your heart may be enlightened, so that you will know what is the hope of His calling, what are the riches of the glory of His inheritance in the saints, ^{19} and what is the boundless greatness of His power toward us who believe. These are in accordance with the working of the strength of His might ^{20} which He brought about in Christ, when He raised Him from the dead and seated Him at His right hand in the heavenly places, ^{21} far above all rule and authority and power and dominion, and every name that is named, not only in this age but also in the one to come. ^{22} And He put all things in subjection under His feet, and made Him head over all things to the church, ^{23} which is His body, the fullness of Him who fills all in all."**
>
> Ephesians 1:15-23

1) In Verse 17, why does Paul want us to have the Spirit of Wisdom & Revelation?

2) He also prays that the "eyes of our heart may be enlightened." Why?

3) According to verses 20-22, Christ is above what?

4) What is Christ's relationship to the church according to verse 22?

5) Who grants our inheritance?
Ephesians 1:14 / Ephesians 5:5 / Hebrews 9:15

> "Inherit" – Merriam-Webster Dictionary
>
> "to come into possession of or receive; especially as a right or divine portion."

6) What do we inherit from God?
Colossians 1:12 / Psalm 2:8 / 1 Peter 1:3-4

7) When do we get this inheritance?   Colossians 3:24

What we have just covered is a quick review of what we have already learned. Jesus Christ is the Head of the Church. He gives us ALL the power, and ALL the authority, along with the KEYS we need, to accomplish that which He commands us to do.

Now that we know we have entered the Kingdom of God through the Gate (Jesus) and have the Family Name, along with access to the Treasures of Heaven, Authority, and Power also granted, and admittance to the Armory, what do we do?

As Jesus was about to ascend into heaven, He gave this directive; we often refer to as the Great Commission.

> "But the eleven disciples proceeded to Galilee, to the mountain which Jesus had designated to them. [17] And when they saw Him, they worshiped Him; but some were doubtful. [18] And Jesus came up and spoke to them, saying, "All authority in heaven and on earth has been given to Me. [19] Go, therefore, and make disciples of all the nations, baptizing them in the name of the Father and the Son and the Holy Spirit, [20] teaching them to follow all that I commanded you; and behold, I am with you always, to the end of the age."
>
> Matthew 28:16-20

8) How much authority does Jesus have?

9) How far does this authority extend?

Jesus said to go make disciples of all nations . . . let us look at this word translated "make disciples."

> mathēteuō - math-ayt-yoo'-o
>
> To become a pupil; to disciple, that is, enroll as scholar: - be a disciple, instruct, teach.

Jesus is saying that we need to be students first, and in turn, share what we know, creating other students, or as it is translated, disciples. We learn as we follow Jesus, and we invite others to learn and follow along with us! It is that simple!

We also "baptize them in the name of the Father and of the Son and of the Holy Spirit."

> baptizō - bap-tid'-zo
>
> To make whelmed (fully wet); used only (in the New Testament) of ceremonial ablution, especially of the ordinance of Christian baptism; to cover wholly with a fluid; in a qualified or specific sense, that is, (literally) to moisten (a part of one's person), to stain as with dye.

We get the sense that part of what Jesus is communicating here is that our teaching involves immersing our students in the knowledge and experience of the Father, Son, and Holy Spirit.

An act of baptism in the river or baptistery is an outward profession of something already taking place inside the heart!

We are to teach them to obey everything Jesus commanded. Look at the word we translate as "OBEY."

> tēreō - tay-reh'-o
>
> To guard from loss by keeping the eye upon; hold fast.

We must hold fast to the teachings of Jesus, following His directives, and teaching others to do the same. We must avail ourselves of the words preserved in the Bible.

A great starting place is Matthew 5-7, the Sermon on the Mount, and studying the words of Jesus throughout the New Testament.

One more thing before we conclude this study. What exactly did Jesus do that compelled the people to want to be disciples in the first place? Well, here it is . . .

> "And He came to Nazareth, where He had been brought up; and as was His custom, He entered the synagogue on the Sabbath, and stood up to read. [17] And the scroll of Isaiah the prophet was handed to Him. And He unrolled the scroll and found the place where it was written: [18] "The Spirit of the Lord is upon Me, because He anointed Me to bring good news to the poor. He has sent Me to proclaim release to captives, and recovery of sight to the blind, to set free those who are oppressed, [19] to proclaim the favorable year of the Lord."
>
> [20] And He rolled up the scroll, gave it back to the attendant, and sat down; and the eyes of all the people in the synagogue were intently directed at Him. [21] Now He began to say to them, "Today this Scripture has been fulfilled in your hearing."
>
> Luke 4:16-21

As maturing disciples of Jesus, we are to do what Jesus did. As you begin to unravel the brokenness of this world, reaching people for Jesus, loving them, touching them, healing them, releasing them, you can be sure that the enemy of your soul will do all he can to stop your activities.

Take courage, you have all the **Right Equipment**, you have the **Keys** to it all, and you access it all through prayer... from where you really live; from the **Upside Down**. We are to do the very things detailed in the passage Jesus read that day!

In light of what we have learned through these studies, our life of prayer takes on new meaning and power. God has granted us access to Him through Jesus, and when we pray, we engage God Himself.

When we pray, we talk to the **God** of this universe, our **Creator**, our **Sustainer**, the **Captain of the Lord's Army**! Assigned by Him to advance **His Kingdom** here on earth until Jesus returns, our prayer life takes on a new perspective; we pray believing, expecting, and advancing His cause.

We no longer doubt or waffle in our prayer, because we come to the throne of grace with boldness and assurance.

It is my earnest prayer that you would keep the truths you have learned through this Bible study near to your heart; revisit them frequently, stay sharp and aware of the amazing spiritual truths revealed to you. Armed with these truths, you are ready to engage! **Call out to your Heavenly Father boldly** and with assurance; He hears you and will act on your behalf! You are a **Complete Christian**, lacking nothing; you are equipped, fully armored; now advance the **Kingdom of God**!

Remember, and never forget your position with Christ; it is in the heavenly realms; operate from there, and pray... **Upside ~ Down**!

Notes:

Facilitating an Effective Small Group

Pray for each member of your small group throughout the week. The goal of your small group is about learning the Word of God together; it is also about sharing life, beyond the context of the weekly meeting.

Take time to preview the lesson ahead of time, anticipating group responses and considering points of discussion. Take time to pray for God to open hearts and minds to the spiritual truths about to be revealed.

Start and stop the meeting promptly at the designated times, honoring those who arrive on schedule, and allowing those who may have a babysitter or other obligations to leave the group without feeling awkward.

Start the meeting with an icebreaker; ask the group to answer a safe, revealing question: What is your favorite dessert, who was your childhood superhero, where were you born, etc.

Avoid doing all the speaking in the group; participation from each member is the goal.

Be the first to share your heart when difficult and sensitive discussions come up, opening the door for others to share too. It is okay to be vulnerable.

If you do not know the answer to a specific question, be candid and let the group know that you do not know the answer, but that you will do your best to find the answer and bring it next week.

Portions of this study are intense and may cause uncomfortable moments. Be sure to treat those moments prayerfully, with great care and compassion.

Finally, enjoy the journey with your small group, get together after the study is over; do a prayer event, or a fun activity together.

ABOUT THE AUTHOR – Rock Pifer

Raised in a small rural community in North Central Pennsylvania, Rock enjoyed country life, which included motorcycles, hiking, hunting, fishing, and camping. When Rock reached his teen years, he began to dabble in drugs and alcohol, which led to an unhealthy desire for more. By the time he was 17 years old, he had a real problem.

In 1979, he met his future wife, Sherri. The two ran away to Ohio and began an unholy life together, one of drugs, alcohol, stealing, and a host of other poor life choices. Sherri became pregnant, and Rock and Sherri moved back to Pennsylvania.

In the fall of 1989, a local church began reaching out to this troubled couple. The church convinced Rock to let the two children they now had come to Sunday School.

In the summer of 1990, Rock and Sherri grudgingly went to a church Camp meeting, and there, on a hot July night, they both met Jesus, and a life transformation took place.

In two short years, Rock would begin pursuing ordained ministry, and in 1995, Rock became pastor of the church that helped lead him to Christ. Rock and Sherri would serve that church, along with two other churches, for nearly 25 years.

Today, both Rock and Sherri are ordained pastors, serving as evangelists, preaching in churches, and sharing a powerful message of hope and transformation.

www.ingramcontent.com/pod-product-compliance
Lightning Source LLC
Chambersburg PA
CBHW081401070526
44583CB00020B/2631